LAUNCH OUT

FRANK OVEC

authorHOUSE®

AuthorHouse™
1663 Liberty Drive
Bloomington, IN 47403
www.authorhouse.com
Phone: 833-262-8899

Published by AuthorHouse 10/26/2023

ISBN: 978-1-5462-0653-8 (sc)
ISBN: 978-1-5462-0651-4 (hc)
ISBN: 978-1-5462-0652-1 (e)

Library of Congress Control Number: 2017913390

Print information available on the last page.

CONTENTS

CHAPTER 1

WHAT MUST I DO?

What is the right thing to do? Whenever a person becomes old enough to grow aware of his or her own use of reason, this question must arise. Why am I here?[1] Why was I born into this world, existing with so many others, all captivated by this same awareness? What must I do? I believe in my existence. I'm aware that "I am." I must be a relative of God, who also said, "I am."[2] I believe it's true, then. I am from God.[3] I am also aware that there is a certain inborn luminosity that draws my heart away from darkness like a moth.[4] I reach for this light, but I can't grasp it. I desire it, but it eludes me. What must I do to achieve this light? What is it?

According to John's gospel, the answer is "True Light." This "True Light" shines in the darkness and illuminates every person who is born into the world.[5]

The Hebrew rendition of the term "True Light" means a covenant light, or an established, promised light.[6]

In Jeremiah chapter 31, the prophet announces that God has instituted a new covenant with mankind[7] because the old covenant, which contained laws and commandments inscribed in stone and written in pen, was hostile to mankind and easily broken and forgotten. In the new covenant, God has placed the sum of the law within our minds and within our hearts. There He has inscribed it. In this way, a communion with God is inherently understood.[8]

As John the Baptist preached repentance from dark

works, many people asked about the fruits of repentance, saying, "What must I do?" These people were both Jews and Gentiles (non-Jewish).[9] John therefore expressed this notion to them: "Do good works." It becomes evident then that doing good works is an outward sign that favors salvation.[10]

It has been said (and rightly so) that doing good works is not salvation. Jesus is salvation. Nevertheless, let us not downsize the concept of good works before salvation.

Because of this new covenant, which has become an inherent Light to all of mankind, good works are working. However, evil works continue to work too because not every person shall be drawn from darkness unto the Light.[11] Some hate the Light and will never come to the Light. But everyone who practices the works of True Light comes to the Light, proving that he or she has been fashioned by God, whose workmanship continues according to a predestined and timely salvation.[12]

Remember that Jesus said, "No one can come to me unless the father who sent me draws him."[13]

Salvation is an honor and a great privilege. It clearly belongs to the Lord,[14] and His desire is for you. So to answer the question "What must I do?" keep working the good works of God, and wait expectantly for His salvation.[15]

References for Chapter 1

1   Romans 1:19–20.

2   Exodus 3:14.

3   John 1:3. Colossians 1:16–17.

4   John 1:4, 9.

5   John 1:1–9.

6   Strong's Exhaustive Concordance, Compact Edition, James H. Strong, Baker Book House, Grand Rapids, Michigan, 1984.Pg. 14 of Hebrew dictionary #559–662. A Complete Hebrew And English Critical And Pronouncing Dictionary, 2nd Edition, William L. Roy, John F. Trow & Co., New York, N.Y. 1846.Pg. 36–37.

7   Jeremiah 31:31–34.

8   Romans 2:14–15.

9   Luke 3:8–14.

10 Ephesians 2:10.

11 John 3:19–20.

12 John 3:21. Ephesians 1:11, 2:10.

13 John 6:44, 65.

14 Psalm 3:8.

15 Micah 7:7. 1 Timothy 2:3–4. 2 Peter 3:9.

CHAPTER 2

WHAT DID JESUS SAY?

The counsel from John the Baptist truly challenges the inquisitive heart, but what did Jesus say?

In the third chapter of the gospel of John (not the Baptist), Nicodemus, a Jewish ruler and teacher in Israel, came to Jesus by night. He came seeking a deeper understanding about the truth in the words of Jesus. He was already aware of the fact that Jesus was sent from God because of His miraculous deeds. It was then that Jesus told him what he must do. He said, "You must be born again."[1] That means being born of the water and of the spirit. Without this, no one can enter the kingdom of God.

Nicodemus did not understand this rebirth concept. "What does it mean to be born of the water and of the spirit?" he asked.[2] He could understand only earthly things, such as being born in the flesh. However, Jesus was not talking about earthly things but about heavenly things—things of the spirit. And the spirit, being compared to the wind that blows in all directions according to the will of God, cannot be seen,[3] but the sound of its testimony is evident by those who declare it.[4]

References for Chapter 2

1 John 3:3–7.

2 John 3:9.

3 John 3:7–8.

4 Psalm 19:1–4.

CHAPTER 3

BEING BORN OF THE WATER

I n order to begin our studies of "being born of the water," we must first determine what the meaning of the word *water* is. It is first seen in the Book of Genesis and last seen in the Book of Revelation.[1] It is used hundreds of times throughout the Bible, but whether singular or plural in form, and whether found in the Old Testament or in the New Testament, the word *water* is derived from the same Hebrew word, *mayim*, which means the springs or semen of the water of life.[2]

This indicates a rudimentary substance for biological life that has evolved into molecular DNA within the seed of mankind.

As discussed earlier, some people refuse to accept True Light, which is given by God to illuminate the waters of life within mankind.[3] These people love the works of darkness and therefore hate the Light, and they will never come to the Light.[4] And there are those who love the existence of True Light and come to the Light, exhibiting a life of Light.[5] Herein is the difference between darkness (which indicates a spiritual countenance of sorrow and death) and Light (which indicates a spiritual countenance of joy at the birth of life).[6]

In the fourth chapter of the gospel of John, we see Jesus talking to a Gentile woman at a well in the city of Samaria. He indicates to her that He is the source of water that gives everlasting life, and that the men she is associated with are not the source of water that gives everlasting life.

In a subtle way, Jesus is saying to her that He is her true husband, for the waters (lineage) of the Gentiles do not bring forth salvation as a resurrection from eternal death to eternal life; for salvation is of the Jews.[7]

This same concept is recognized in the gospel of Mark.[8] Here, Jesus teaches that ultimately God is the promise of eternal life, which exists within the living seed of Abraham, Isaac, and Jacob.[9]

And so it is that the true water of the Spirit of life that was breathed into Adam flows through the seed of Abraham, Isaac, and Jacob and unto Jesus the Jew.[10]

The woman at the well was not a Jew; she was a Gentile. Nevertheless, she expressed her hope of glory according to her faith in the promise of salvation, which was also allotted to the Gentiles and foretold by the prophets of old.[11]

So how does the promise of living water, which is to spring up throughout a people who are not Jewish, come to fruition?

Consider the story of Ruth from the Book of Ruth.

Ruth's lineage came from Moab, the son of Lot, the nephew to Abraham. She was not a direct descendant of Abraham in whose seed (Isaac) the blessings of glory belong. Nevertheless, after her husband died, Ruth attached herself to her mother-in-law, Naomi, whose lineage was of the seed of Abraham, being manifested within the tribe of Judah of the sons of Jacob, also known as Israel.[12]

As the story unfolds, Ruth refuses to leave Naomi and maintains her position in saying, "Where you go, I will go and where you live, I will live. Your people will be my people and your God will be my God. Where you die and are buried, there will I die and be buried."[13]

In this case, the faith of Ruth was established because of her love for Naomi and her descent.[14] Ruth, therefore, through faith, became a proselyte to the Jews, seeking a city greater than her own.[15]

To answer the question of how the promise of living water springs up into all of the families of the earth, it is by faith. However, it is not by faith in the Jewish people but by faith in our Creator, who promised it.[16]

In New Testament times (after the coming of Jesus), Paul received his ministry as an apostle to the Gentiles by the spirit of revelation when he met Jesus on the road to Damascus.[17]

In his letter to the Romans, Paul sums up Gentile salvation in the following. By faith, the Gentiles become grafted into the vine of Adam, which extends throughout Abraham, Isaac, and Jacob, from which came forth Israel unto Jesus the Jew.[18] Don't forget salvation is of the Jews.[19]

And so it is that the Gentiles become spiritual Jews, being reborn by faith into the seed of Abraham, who is of the vine of Adam.

Because Jesus is the end and the fulfillment of the promise of salvation to all of the families of the earth; everyone—whether male or female, Jew or Gentile— who belongs to Him takes on the seed of Abraham and becomes joint heirs of the promise of the glory of salvation.[20]

In retrospect, as Ruth by faith accepted the Lord (Jehovah) God of all creation in Old Testament times, so do people by faith accept the Lord God of all creation in New Testament times.

Whether Jew or Gentile, the outward sign of one who belongs to the Lord God in Old Testament times is the covenant of circumcision, which involves the cutting of the flesh. The outward sign of one who belongs to the Lord God in New Testament times is the covenant of baptism, which involves being submerged in water.[21]

Ruth, being a woman, did not undergo circumcision, which was administered to all males who were to become the heads of every household in Hebrew history. Nevertheless, it has become evident that favor was shown to her by God in opposition to the law of the covenant of circumcision.

Therefore, in the story of Ruth, the sign of the covenant of circumcision, which by law necessitates the cutting of the flesh in order to be considered as "belonging to the Lord," was overruled by her faith in the promise that was given to Abraham for all of mankind, whether male or female, Jew or Gentile.[22]

Conversely, the sign of the covenant of salvation, which by law necessitates being submerged in water, is overruled by a lack of faith and good works, which are associated with repentance and turning to God.[23]

John the Baptist emphatically expressed this to everyone who came to him to be baptized, admonishing them to bring forth fruits worthy of repentance and acceptance by God. He went so far as to call the so-called leaders and teachers in Israel a brood of vipers.[24]

With all this in mind, it becomes evident that neither circumcision nor baptism amounts to salvation, for God looks at the spirit in the heart.[25]

This concept of the spirit in the heart, leads us to the next and final step to being born again, and that is "being born of the spirit." This spirit is the Holy Spirit that comes to us as a latter rain and is separate from the early rain, which is associated with "being born of the water."[26]

In explanation, there are two ways in which the spirit of living waters comes to us. At first, the living waters come to us as an early rain in which the Spirit of Jesus is "with" us. Second, the living waters come to us as a latter rain in which the Spirit of Jesus is "in" us.[27]

This concept of the Spirit in us takes us to the next chapter, fulfilling the requirements of being born again.

References for Chapter 3

1 Genesis 1:2. Revelation 22:17.

2 Strong's Exhaustive Concordance, Compact Edition, James H. Strong, Baker Book House, Grand Rapids, Michigan, 1984.Pg. 65 of Hebrew dictionary #4325. A Complete Hebrew And English Critical And Pronouncing Dictionary, 2nd Edition, William L. Roy, John F. Trow & Co., New York, N.Y. 1846.Pg. 291,449.

3 Genesis 1:1–5. John 1:9.

4 John 1:5, 3:19–20.

5 John 3:21. 1 John 1:5–7.

6 John 4:24, 6:63, 17:13. Matthew 2:10.

7 Isaiah 9:6–7, 54:4–5. Micah 5:2. John 4:22.

8 Mark 12:19–27.

9 A Complete Hebrew And English Critical And Pronouncing Dictionary, 2nd Edition, William L. Roy, John F. Trow & Co., New York, N.Y. 1846.Pg.

30. (Elah, as God the promise). Colossians 1:27. 2 Timothy 1:1.

10 Genesis 2:7.

11 Genesis 12:3, 17:1–4, 18:18, 22:18, 26:4, 28:14. Isaiah 11:10, 42:1–8, 49:6, 22.

12 Genesis 35:10.

13 Ruth 1:16–17.

14 Genesis 15:1–6. Galatians 5:6.

15 Hebrews 11:14–16.

16 Genesis 12:3, 15:6. Mark 11:22.

17 Acts 9.

18 John 15:1–5. Romans 11:13–24.

19 John 4:22.

20 Romans 8:15–18. Galatians 3:28–29.

21 Genesis 17:10–14. Matthew 3:13–15.

22 Genesis 15:6, 22:18. Galatians 3:7–9, 28, 5:6.

23 Mark 16:16. John 3:5,19–21. Ephesians 2:8–10.

24 Genesis 4:3–7. Matthew 3:1–8. Luke 3:7–8.

25 1 Samuel 16:7. Romans 2:28–29.

26 Hosea 6:3. Joel 2:23. Zechariah 10:1. John 1:33, 3:5. James 5:7–8.

27 John 14:15–17. 2 Thessalonians 1:10.

CHAPTER 4

BEING BORN OF THE SPIRIT

After His resurrection, Jesus appeared to as many as five hundred early church Christians with encouraging words and visions.[1] His instruction was to wait for the promise of the Holy Spirit, which in time would be given, as a latter rain to all who believe in the gospel (good news) of everlasting life.[2] Remember, it is the spirit that gives life.[3] How much more, then, is the latter rain of the Holy Spirit to abound in life for those who receive it?

It is a thing of faith to be born of the spirit. It doesn't always happen immediately. I have learned this myself because it took months before the manifestation of the Holy Spirit was evident in me.[4] In fact, I didn't even know that there was a Holy Spirit until the night of the encounter. It was like turning on a light bulb in a dark room, and I haven't been the same since. Everyone knew that something was different.

On the night of that encounter, I was drifting away from the early rain of my spiritual awakening. I was losing my grip on life in more ways than one, but the goodness and patience of God abounded to glory in me. The next day, I was carrying a Bible, which was very peculiar indeed.[5] I haven't missed a day of reading from it since. I consider the Bible a roadmap through life. I don't see how anyone can make it to a fair haven on earth without the guiding light of God's word.[6]

With all this said, I can testify that it was my rudimentary faith, in expectation that something good was going to happen, that rose my life up from the dead. Therefore I say to you, wait for the gift of the Holy Spirit and don't give up.[7]

Consider the parable of the sower and the seed, which was taught by Jesus and documented in Three Gospels.[8]

The seed that is sown is the word of truth and the ground upon which it is cast is the heart of mankind.[9] In short, if the ground is bad, it will not produce fruit; if the ground is good, in time it will produce fruit. The fruit discussed here is the Holy Spirit.[10]

The people of the world, who are not first and foremost born of the water, cannot be sealed in the Holy Spirit of promise, which is given only to those who believe in God with a sincere heart and have come to know Him through salvation that is in Jesus.[11]

Once a person of the world, who by faith, comes to Jesus, who is not of the world, he or she shall receive an early rain of the Spirit of Jesus, who is to be with them. Those who maintain their faith in Jesus shall receive of the latter rain of the Spirit of Jesus, who is then to be born in them.[12]

In the story of the early church, there were over five hundred souls who had some form of a direct encounter with our risen Savior, Jesus. However, only about one hundred and twenty were in the upper room on the day of the rushing mighty wind.[13]

It is evident that even after an acceptance of truth that is in Jesus is made, certain powers of temptation that are associated with the former way of life can cause a person to fall away. How good is the ground?

It all boils down to our faith because the victory that overcomes the powers of temptation is our faith.[14]

God loves faith because without faith it is impossible to please Him.[15] A person must first believe that God exists as the great "I Am" and therefore accepts the love of the truth that is in Jesus,[16] which is being "born of the water." Through diligent faith, the gift of the Holy Spirit is to be rewarded within us, which is being "born of the spirit." It is the knowledge of this truth that shall set us free from powers of temptation.[17]

Remember, greater is He who is in you than he who is the world.[18]

Even though temptations will come and sometimes sin follows, nothing shall separate us from the love of God that is in Christ Jesus our Lord.[19] We have come to know the grace and truth that is in Jesus, our Intercessor. If we confess our sins, He is faithful and just to forgive us of our sins and to cleanse us from all unrighteousness.[20]

Therefore, it is our persistent faith that brings us into the concept of salvation, being "born again."[21]

Consider what Jesus teaches in the gospel of Mark. "He that believes and is baptized shall be saved." "He that does not believe shall be condemned."[22]

Once again, be not confused. Neither the cutting of the flesh as circumcision nor being submerged in water as baptism is necessary for salvation. The necessity is accepting the love of the truth that is in Jesus because God looks at the heart.

In paraphrase of this passage, the concept of "to believe" is to accept the love of the truth that is in Jesus, who comes to us as living water—thereby being "born of the water." The concept of "to be baptized" is to be infilled with the Holy Spirit, which follows belief—thereby being "born of the Spirit."[23]

References for Chapter 4

1 1 Corinthians 15:6.

2 Strong's Exhaustive Concordance, Compact Edition, James H. Strong, Baker Book House, Grand Rapids, Michigan, 1984.Pg. 24 of Hebrew dictionary #1308–9; Greek dictionary #2097–8. Acts 1:4–8.

3 John 6:63.

4 Romans 15:18.

5 Titus 2:14(KJV). 1 Peter 2:9 (KJV).

6 Psalm 107:30, 119:105. Proverbs 4:18–19, 6:23. Isaiah 43:16.

7 Acts 2:38–39.

8 Matthew 13. Mark 4. Luke 8.

9 John 17:17.

10 John 14:17. Ephesians 5:9.

11 John 17:3. Ephesians 1:13.

12 John 8:23, 14:17.

13 Acts 1:4–9, 15. 1 Corinthians 15:6.

14 Colossians 1:21–23. 1 John 5:4.

15 Hebrews 11:6.

16 John 8:58.

17 John 8:31–36, 14:17. 2 Corinthians 3:17.

18 Luke 10:19. 1 John 4:4.

19 Luke 4:13, 22:28. Romans 8:35–39.

20 1 John 1:9, 2:1.

21 John 3:3–5.

22 Mark 16:16.

23 Luke 3:16.

CHAPTER 5

RISING IN REBIRTH

Know this: that by accepting Jesus into our own character, we become baptized into His death and consequently into His life, according to the power of His resurrection.[1]

This is the rebirth process by which we are being transformed into His character as new creations known as the body of Christ upon the earth.[2] So how does this work?

A fact of biological life is that it ends in death, which

is the result of sin. Sin is a self-centered rebellion due to disbelief in the word of God.[3] This first occurred at the fall of Satan and is known as the great transgression.[4]

Satan, who is known as the son of the morning, is actually the first of God's creations under His right-hand nature. The right-hand nature of God is known as the bright and morning star, Jesus.[5] The cosmos followed in glorious rays of light without tangible form until Satan left his first estate, which was to guard against the advancement of darkness that was below the surface of the deep.[6] In a presumptuous manner, he exalted his position to the height of God. As a result, the cosmos became corrupted and took form under the burden of darkness that crept above the surface of the deep.[7] It was through this corruption of darkness that biological flesh took form. Then God said, "Let there be light," which is the True Light. The True Light shined in the darkness and separated Satan from the height of God to a domain below the surface of the deep.[8] And God called the light "Day," which by His

Spirit Illumines the waters of life. To the gathering of darkness, God called it "Night," which by Hebrew definition means "A twisting spiral staircase," which we now understand to be deoxyribonucleic acid (DNA).[9]

Therefore because of the fall of Satan, which affected the form of the waters of life, it becomes evident that all biological life (DNA) is destined to corruption under the darkness of death. Nevertheless, God sent the True Light of His right-hand nature, Jesus, into the world, inhabiting a body of flesh that is also destined to death.[10]

Because Jesus is God incarnate, He knew no sin.[11] Yet upon His death, which is the character of the world, He descended to the bottom of hell, where Satan's seat is. Because darkness and death cannot fellowship with the Light of God, Satan could not keep Him there. As a result, Jesus was cast out from darkness and rose up from the dead.

This concept of an uncontested resurrection is why all who abide in Jesus have eternal life.

Consider the passage in Isaiah 53:11. In this passage,

according to Masoretic Hebrew, we have this: "After the grief of His soul, He shall see Light and be satisfied. By His experience, my righteous servant shall justify many for He shall bear their sin."

If we as a people of this world become united in Jesus, who carries our iniquities, then upon His resurrection, the power of death and sorrows of hell are left behind.

This same concept is found working within the existing body of Christ upon the earth. By our experiences, we are able to bear the burdens of others who are weak in faith. If we can rise in Light, so can they.

A key word in this passage is *many* because many is not everyone. Therefore, not everyone will be saved from the darkness of sin and death. Nevertheless, the salvation message of good news is given to all.

Remember the parable of the sower and the seed.[12] Once again, how good is the ground? All you have to do is believe; and don't give up. The Light of life is coming.[13]

References for Chapter 5

1 Romans 6:3–5. Philippians 3:10. Colossians 2:12.

2 2 Corinthians 5:17.

3 John 16:9. Romans 6:23.

4 Psalm 19:13. Luke 10:18.

5 Isaiah 14:12. John 1:1–3. Colossians 1:16–17. Revelation 22:16.

6 Genesis 1:1–2. Habakkuk 3:4. Jude 6.

7 Genesis 1:2.

8 Genesis 1:2–4. Isaiah 14:12-15.

9 Strong's Exhaustive Concordance, Compact Edition, James H. Strong, Baker Book House, Grand Rapids, Michigan,1984.Pg. 59 of Hebrew dictionary #3883,3915. Biology The Unity And Diversity Of Life, 3rd Edition, Starr and Taggart, Wadsworth Publishing Co., Belmont, California,1984 Pg. 192–203.

10 John 1:1–3, 14. 1 John 4:2. 2 John 7.

11 John 10:30. 2 Corinthians 5:21.

12 Matthew 13. Mark 4. Luke 8.

13 Isaiah 60:1–3. John 1:7–12, 3:16–21, 6:63, 12:35–36, 14:11.

CHAPTER 6

THE GIFTS OF THE SPIRIT

I t is the spirit that gives life, but the outward sign of being baptized in the Holy Spirit is the reception of spiritual gifts.

Some have received gifts as apostles, prophets, evangelists, pastors, or teachers. Some have received gifts of prophecy, healing, faith, working of miracles, helps, or administrations. Some have received gifts of discerning of spirits, the word of wisdom and knowledge, diversity of tongues, interpretation of tongues, and whatever else is given for the edification of the body of Christ, which are the believers in Jesus.[1]

The key word here is *edification,* which means "to build up or strengthen."[2]

Every Christian has his or her own personal and edifying testimony that seals belief in God through Jesus, His Son. This is the account of my testimony.[3]

On Easter Sunday night in 1973, I was traveling on a road in northern Ohio. Suddenly a great light of awesome beauty and extreme glory appeared before me toward the eastern sky. I was filled with an overflowing joy that only one word could describe: love. Three times that word came forth from my mouth in an uncontrolled manner as I beheld the vision. It was in this encounter that I clearly met the love of God in the personage of Jesus Christ.

Being prompted by that vision, I write these words to build up the body of Christ into the love of the truth.[4]

I don't see the word *writer* listed among the spiritual gifts, but I know that I am to write. I remember what

Paul said: "Woe is me if I don't preach the good news." I say, "Woe is me if I don't write."[5]

Whether you have the gift of the early rain of the Holy Spirit of faith, or the latter rain of the Holy Spirit of baptism, use your gift. It's there.

The least of the gifts of the Holy Spirit of baptism and the most talked about is the gift of tongues.[6] There are two kinds of tongues. One is to edify the church body, and one is to edify oneself. In the first kind of tongues, within an assembly of the church body, the Holy Spirit will speak through a gifted individual with an unusual utterance. This will happen with a gifted interpreter present; otherwise, no one would be edified.[7]

Keep in mind that the Spirit is selective, moving throughout the church body as He wills.[8] For example, in a very large body of believers, the gift of tongues and interpretation will not be effective because not everyone will hear. That would be confusion, and God is not the author of confusion.[9]

In the second kind of tongues, the Holy Spirit will

speak through a gifted individual with an unusual utterance that is accepted by God in a personal way. It is designed to relieve an unknown burden of the heart. The edification here is for the individual member of the body of Christ.[10]

Whenever I become burdened about something that I know nothing about, I pray in an utterance of words that I know nothing about. In practice, I have learned that a certain virtue is being released, as it were, to God, and the burden dissipates. It works, and so peace follows. It simply feels right.

Once again, all these words are written according to what I have learned by experience. I will not dare to speak of anything except for what God has purposed in me.[11]

In retrospect, the purpose of these spiritual gifts is to build up the church body into the fullness of God through the love of the truth.[12] Nevertheless, the fullness of God and His glory is not yet visible, and so now we see dimly as it were. Yet through spiritual edification, our inner man is being enlightened more and more, day by day.[13] However, when the fullness of the love of God comes at the return of Jesus, who is to be glorified in us, edification through spiritual gifts will cease, because we shall be like Him, seeing clearly and understanding all things.[14]

References for Chapter 6

1 1 Corinthians 12:8–10, 28–30. Ephesians 4:11–13.

2 Strong's Exhaustive Concordance, Compact Edition, James H. Strong, Baker Book House, Grand Rapids, Michigan, 1984.Pg. 51 of Greek dictionary, #3618–3620.

3 John 3:33. (KJV).

4 John 14:6. Ephesians 4:11–16.

5 1 Corinthians 9:16.

6 Mark 16:17. Acts 10:44–46. 1 Corinthians 14:1–5.

7 1 Corinthians 14:5.

8 1 Corinthians 12:11.

9 1 Corinthians 14:33.

10 Romans 8:26–27. Jude 20–21.

11 Romans 15:18.

12 Ephesians 3:14–19, 4:11–16. Colossians 1:18–19, 2:8–9.

13 2 Corinthians 4:13–18.

14 1 Corinthians 13:8–13. 2 Thessalonians 1:10. 1 John 3:2.

CHAPTER 7

QUEST FOR THE HOLY SPIRIT

Upon accepting Jesus Christ as your personal Savior, you have become baptized into His death and consequently into His resurrection.[1] Nevertheless, the baptism in the Holy Spirit, which resurrects life from the dead, is not always immediate. The promise of the baptism in the Spirit is to all who believe even in His very name.[2] And so it is that we who continue in belief can be rest assured that the Spirit of God through

Jesus, who is with us shall resurrect life within us. And if God be with us, who can be against us?[3]

Let us press on to maturity beyond the rudimentary principles of early salvation, such as repentance, water immersion, fasting, and other such sacrifices that God will use to test the sincerity of our faith.[4]

Once these elementary works have been approved, let us press on in faith to the fullness of God's promise without fear, waiting in great expectation for the baptism in the Holy Spirit of life, at which time this same spirit who is with us shall be in us.[5]

Remember that greater is He who is in you than he who is in the world.[6] It becomes evident that the Holy Spirit shall surely strengthen us against the temptations of the devil.[7]

It is a wise thing, then, to request of God for the baptism of the Holy Spirit, which brings strength and great joy to the believer.[8] It is for this reason that Jesus encourages us to ask.[9] He goes on to say that if we as parents, who are not to be compared to the goodness of

God, can give good gifts unto our children, then how much more shall our heavenly Father give the Holy Spirit to those who request of Him for it?[10]

We are all sheep of God's pasture with a niche in the body of Christ, and the chief shepherd of course is Jesus.[11] Nevertheless, through the zeal of the Holy Spirit of baptism, He has chosen unto Himself those to be shepherds of the sheep of His flock.[12] Even so, whether we are poor in spirit or rich in spirit, whether we are leaders or followers, we are all unconditionally loved by the same God, who has called us to be joint heirs to the kingdom of heaven because of our faith in Jesus.[13] Remember this: blessed are the meek and those poor in spirit, for they shall inherit the kingdom of heaven upon the earth when Jesus returns.[14]

It is God's delight to share the kingdom with His children; and it is because of His delight that we prosper in both body and soul.[15] Therefore if our souls take delight in knowing Him, He will give us the desires of our hearts.[16]

This word *give*, according to the Hebrew definition, means "add to, cause or apply."[17] If you feel a desire to lead or teach, but you are lacking in courage to carry this out, simply ask God for the baptism in the Holy Spirit that will strengthen your inner man.[18]

Remember that God loves faith, and it takes faith in God to request of Him for anything in prayer.[19] It is as though God is waiting to bless us. Just ask.

As for the meek and those who are weak in spirit, don't worry. When Jesus returns, we shall all receive of the gift of our faith, which is the Spirit of Jesus being glorified within us.[20] At that time, there shall be neither high nor low, nor those rich in spirit, nor those poor in spirit. Every hill shall be brought low, and every valley shall be raised.[21] We shall all be united in the selfsame Spirit of Jesus in that day, for those who endure to the end shall be saved.[22]

References for Chapter 7

1 Romans 6:3–5.

2 John 1:12, 2:23.

3 Romans 8:31.

4 Hebrews 6:1–3.

5 Psalm 40:6. Ecclesiastes 9:7. Habakkuk 2:4. John 14:15–17, 6:63. Acts1:4–5. Ephesians 2:8–9.

6 1 John 4:4.

7 Ephesians 3:14–19, 6:10.

8 Nehemiah 8:10. Psalm 21:1–6.

9 John 16:24.

10 Zechariah 10:1. Luke 11:13.

11 Psalm 23:1, 79:13, 100:3. 1 Corinthians 12:18.

12 Jeremiah 23:4. Luke 3:16. John 15:16, 21:15–17. 1 Peter 5:1–4.

13 Matthew 5:3. Romans 8:17. 2 Timothy 3:14–15.

14 Psalm 37:11. Matthew 5:1–12, 6:10.

15 Luke 12:32. 3 John 2.

16 Psalm 37:4. John 17:3. 2 Timothy 4:8.

17 Strong's Exhaustive Concordance, Compact Edition, James H. Strong, Baker Book House, Grand Rapids, Michigan, 1984.Pg. 81 of Hebrew dictionary, #5414.

18 Zechariah 4:6. Ephesians 3:14–20.

19 Hebrews 11:6.

20 Colossians 1:27. 2 Thessalonians 1:10.

21 Isaiah 40:3–5. Luke 3:4–6.

22 Zechariah 14:9. Mark 13:13. Luke 18:8. Ephesians 4:4–5. 1 Peter 1:9.

CHAPTER 8

A GREAT REVIVAL

When Moses encountered the presence of God at the burning bush, he asked God for a clear understanding as to who He actually was. God answered by saying, "I Am."[1] The Hebrew word for "I Am" is *Haya*, which means "self-existing or is all."[2] Therefore God is the visible and invisible cosmos of both matter and spirit.[3] It is the spirit that affects the hearts and minds of men, so in a subtle way, all of mankind is aware of the life-giving spirit from which it came.[4] Those who have tasted of the early rain of God's Spirit are waiting in earnest expectation for the manifestation of the fullness of the sons of God, when Jesus returns at the end of our present age.[5] And who are the sons of God, but they who have received of the latter rain of God's Spirit within them?[6]

For now, those whose deeds are wrought in God have come to Christ apart from the fashion of this present age, with great expectation for the spirit of glory that is yet to come. And for those whose deeds are not wrought in God, they shall continue within a certain fearful expectation of a judgment that is yet to come.[7]

Nevertheless, whether we as a people of this present age live or die, we shall all stand before the judgment seat of Christ Jesus after He returns.[8]

The good news is this: all who believe in God through Jesus Christ shall not come into judgment, but have passed from the judgment of death into the resurrection of life. Furthermore, those who hear the voice of the Son of God when He returns, shall rise in a massive, worldwide revival, and they shall lead many to salvation in Jesus.[9]

This concept is often termed the Rapture, which is a misnomer that indicates a great snatching away. Remember that Jesus is coming back to set up His kingdom as heaven upon the earth, and we as His resurrected body shall be nowhere apart from that.[10] In fact, He is not taking us out of the world, but rather establishing us as its true inheritors whose deeds are wrought in God.[11] However, that which is to be taken out of the world is the sinners who have refused the love of the truth and whose deeds are not wrought in God.[12]

References for Chapter 8

1 Exodus 3:14.

2 A Complete Hebrew And English Critical And Pronouncing Dictionary, 2nd Edition, William L. Roy, John F. Trow & Co., New York, N.Y. 1846.Pg. 166–167.

3 Colossians 1:16–17, 3:11.

4 Romans 1:20. Hebrews 11:3.

5 Romans 8:19. 2 Thessalonians 1:10.

6 Romans 8:14.

7 Zephaniah 1:14–18. Hebrews 10:27, 30–31.

8 Daniel 7:9–10, 12:1–2. John 5:28–29.

9 Daniel 12:3. John 5:24–25.

10 Daniel 7:13–14. Matthew 5:3–12, 6:10.

11 Matthew 5:5. John 3:21.

12 Isaiah 13:9. Daniel 12:10. Matthew 13:30, 40–43, 49–50.

CHAPTER 9

THE STUDY

As Jesus taught us, there shall be great tribulation in such a way that no flesh would survive unless those days were shortened.[1] Therefore in a short moment, at the seventh and last trumpet sound and with the voice of the archangel Michael, the dead in Christ shall arise first. Then all who remain in Christ and have survived the great tribulation shall be caught up with them to meet the Lord in the clouds of the air. At that time, the body of Christ shall be changed into glory, for living waters shall be poured out upon all flesh whose deeds are wrought in God as a baptism in the Holy Spirit of promise.[2]

Upon studying the Bible passages associated with the resurrection of the body of Christ, this following understanding comes to light. The word *clouds*, found in 1 Thessalonians 4:17, is the same Hebrew word found in Nahum 1:3, which reveals to us that the clouds are the dust of the Lord's feet.

The word *clouds* means "a mysterious anxiety that covers over and also protects."[3] The word *dust* means "wrestling, contention or scourge."[4] The word *feet* means "foot soldiers that follow."[5] The word *air* from the passage in Thessalonians means "glorious appearance of light and zeal of spirit and fire."[6] The words "caught up" mean "accepted or taken in marriage and led as an army."[7]

God is Spirit, and His return shall be a time of great spiritual awakening, a massive worldwide revival, for the latter rain, as the living waters of the Holy Spirit, shall be poured out upon the army of God, His foot soldiers. And we shall fight in those days, for the weak in spirit and of a fearful heart shall be made strong, and we shall all drink of the living waters and be changed.[8]

The Hebrew word for *changed* (1 Cor. 15:51–52) means "to drink or absorb."[9] And in that day, the heavens shall drop down as dew, watering the earth, and with the voice of Michael the archangel, we shall all be changed.[10]

According to Hebrew definition, the word *Michael* means "to drop down as dew, distilling as water like God."[11]

In that day, the mystery of God is to be completed in this: the armies of our future shall come down, our past shall rise up, and we who are alive at that time shall be united with them in the glory of the dew of God. We shall all drink of it and therefore be changed from weakness to power and from shame to glory.[12]

With an immortal spirit that shall come to us as the latter rain of the dew and the power of Michael the archangel, we shall all rise up to fight in that day. And we shall push back the army of Satan at a time known as the Threshing.[13]

After a short period of time, the stage will be set for the final battle between good and evil at a place known as Armageddon. It is here that the last enemy of the army of God, whose name is Death, shall be destroyed.[14]

This final battle is also known as the great marriage supper of God. It will be a time of God's vengeance against all evil, which culminates at Armageddon, also known as the war of the great day of God.[15]

According to Hebrew definition, the word *Armageddon*, which is also denoted as *Har-Magedon*, means "a mountain of rendezvous where all streams flow."[16] It is here that the kingdom of the world is to become the kingdom of Jesus, and we, the saints of glory, shall take possession of this kingdom, which is to be known as heaven on earth.[17]

Before this day, in a time known as the favorable

year of the Lord, when our redemption draws near, we as the saints who have endured to this end shall have risen up and been rewarded as priests and kings and judges upon the earth. Therefore we shall be the judges of all, including the spirit of fallen angels who inhabit the body of men.[18]

The mystery is this: we are Jesus. This concept is known as the body of Christ upon the earth. That's what and who we are, but the fullness of His glory is not yet revealed. So for now, all nations and tongues whose deeds are wrought in God are waiting in eager expectation for the return of His glory, which will be revealed within us. This revelation will institute a unity within the hearts and minds of men known as the marriage of the lamb, for His bride, the Church, has made herself ready.[19]

From that time onward, we shall inherit brightness and judgment. Many who see not shall see, and many who hear not shall hear, for those whose deeds are wrought in God shall surely come to the brightness of our rising, but those whose deeds are not wrought in God shall remain dim and shall not understand.[20] As God our Father has given all judgment to the Son, so also shall we judge between the good and the evil as the lambs and the goats.[21]

As Jesus taught, there will be two people living side by side, and one shall be taken and the other left.[22]

According to the Hebrew definition, the word *taken* means "accepted or taken in marriage, received."[23] The word *left* means "refused, left, abandoned, forsaken, relinquished."[24] This means that Jesus is coming back to be united in marriage with His bride, the Church body, which is the true worshipers of God upon the earth.[25] At that same time, there will be those who do not have on proper wedding garments (good works); these shall be rejected and therefore cast out of the kingdom of Jesus into a place of weeping and gnashing of teeth (great anger).[26]

Furthermore, the word *taken* is also the same Hebrew base word that is found in Genesis 2:21–22. In this passage, God took (accepted) a rib from Adam. The word *rib* means "a side as a deficient adversary."[27] We will discuss this in the next chapter.

References for Chapter 9

1 Matthew 24: 21–22.

2 Isaiah 35:3–10, 44:3. Joel 2:28. Zechariah 14:7–9. John 7:38–39.

3 A Complete Hebrew And English Critical And Pronouncing Dictionary, 2nd Edition, William L. Roy, John F. Trow & Co., New York, N.Y. 1846. Pg. 562.

4 Strong's Exhaustive Concordance, compact Edition, James H. Strong, Baker Book House, Grand Rapids, Michigan, 1984.Pg. 8 of Hebrew dictionary, #79–80. A Complete Hebrew And English Critical And Pronouncing Dictionary, 2nd Edition, William L. Roy, John F. Trow & Co., New York, N.Y. 1846. Pg. 12.

5 Strong's Exhaustive Concordance, Compact Edition, James H. Strong, Baker Book House, Grand Rapids, Michigan, 1984.Pg.107 of Hebrew dictionary, #7272–73. A Complete Hebrew And

English Critical And Pronouncing Dictionary, 2nd Edition, William L. Roy, John F. Trow & Co., New York, N.Y. 1846.Pg. 627.

6 Strong's Exhaustive Concordance, Compact Edition, James H. Strong, Baker Book House, Grand Rapids, Michigan, 1984.Pg. 9 of Hebrew dictionary, #215–19. A Complete Hebrew And English Critical And Pronouncing Dictionary, 2nd Edition, William L. Roy, John F. Trow & Co., New York, N.Y. 1846.Pg. 18 and 60.

7 Strong's Exhaustive Concordance, Compact Edition, James H. Strong, Baker Book House; Grand Rapids, Michigan, 1984.Pg. 60 of Hebrew dictionary, #3947. A Complete Hebrew And English Critical And Pronouncing Dictionary, 2nd Edition, William L. Roy, John F. Trow & Co., New York, N.Y. 1846. Pg. 416.

8 Isaiah 35:3–4, 41:10–16, 44:2–5. Joel 3:9–10. Zechariah 10:1, 4–5. 1 Corinthians 15:51–52.

9 A Complete Hebrew And English Critical And Pronouncing Dictionary, 2nd Edition, William L. Roy, John F. Trow & Co., New York, N.Y. 1846. Pg. 528.

10 Isaiah 45:8. Daniel 12:1–4. Joel 3:18. 1 Thessalonians 4:16. 2 Thessalonians 1:9–10. Revelation 10:1–3, 7, 11:15–17, 18:1–2.

11 Strong's Exhaustive Concordance, Compact Edition, James H. Strong, Baker Book House, Grand Rapids, Michigan, 1984.Pg. 65 of Hebrew dictionary, #4317. A Complete Hebrew And English Critical Pronouncing Dictionary, 2nd Edition, William L. Roy, John F. Trow & Co., New York, N.Y. 1846.Pg. 345 and 448.

12 Deuteronomy 33:2. Joel 2:23–27. Zechariah 14:5–9. 1 Corinthians 15:51–53. 1 Thessalonians 3:13, 4:16–17. Jude 14. Revelation 10:7,19:14.

13 Isaiah 26:19, 41:15–16. Daniel 12:1. Joel 2:18–20, 3:9–10. Micah 4:13.Zechariah 10:3–5.

14 Isaiah 25:6–8. Daniel 11:44–45. Revelation 6:7–8, 11:15–18, 16:15–17.

15 Deuteronomy 32:35. Revelation 16:13–17, 17:14, 19:9–18.

16 Revelation 16:16(NASB). Strong's Exhaustive Concordance, Compact Edition, James H. Strong, Baker Book House, Grand Rapids, Michigan, 1984. Pg. 61 of Hebrew dictionary, #4023. A Complete Hebrew And English Critical And Pronouncing Dictionary, 2nd Edition, William L. Roy, John F. Trow & Co., New York, N.Y. 1846.Pg. 431.

17 Daniel 7:18, 21–22, 26–27. Matthew 5:3–12. 2 Thessalonians 1:10. Revelation 11:15–18.

18 Isaiah 61:1–2, 63:4. Matthew 10:22. Luke 21:17–28, 22:28–30. 1 Corinthians 6:2–3. Revelation 1:6–7, 5:9–10, 16:13–14.

19 Romans 8:18–19, 12:4–5. 1 Corinthians 12:27. Ephesians 5:30. Revelation 19:7–8.

20 Psalm 97:11(NASB). Isaiah 35:3–10, 60:1–3. Daniel 12:3, 10.

21 Matthew 25:31–46. John 5:22. 1 Corinthians 6:2–3.

22 Matthew 24:40–41. Luke 17:34–35.

23 Strong's Exhaustive Concordance, Compact Edition, James H. Strong, Baker Book House, Grand Rapids, Michigan, 1984.Pg. 60 of Hebrew dictionary, #3947. A Complete Hebrew And English Critical And Pronouncing Dictionary, 2nd Edition, William L. Roy, John F. Trow & Co., New York, N.Y. 1846. Pg. 416.

24 Strong's Exhaustive Concordance. Compact Edition, James H. Strong, Baker Book House, Grand Rapids, Michigan, 1984.Pg. 86 of Hebrew dictionary, #5800. A complete Hebrew And English Critical And Pronouncing Dictionary, 2nd Edition, William L. Roy, John F. Trow & Co., New York, N.Y. 1846.Pg. 550.

25 John 4:23.

26 Matthew 22:1–13, 24:48–51. Revelation 19:7–9.

27 Strong's Exhaustive Concordance, Compact Edition, James H. Strong, Baker Book House, Grand Rapids,

Michigan, 1984.Pg. 100 of Hebrew dictionary, #6761. A Complete Hebrew And English Critical And Pronouncing Dictionary, 2nd Edition, William L. Roy, John F. Trow & Co., New York, N.Y. 1846. Pg. 598.

CHAPTER 10

LAUNCH OUT

I have determined that all people are searching for the truth, even if they don't believe it. That is because everyone has come into existence by and through the truth; it's inherent within us.[1]

To know the truth and the end of a matter is important to us. This is why we maintain progressive research in order to gain knowledge throughout our educational systems. As Christians who claim to know the truth, we need to bear witness of the truth.[2]

Remember that we are fishers of men.[3] It's time to catch the big fish. These are our kings, rulers, and leaders of men; our scientists and teachers; and all skeptics who need to understand the truth in order to believe it.

"Launch out into the deep." These are the words of encouragement from Jesus. Upon obeying these words, great fish were caught by His disciples.[4] Now, this word *deep* is the same Hebrew word that is found in the passage of 1 Corinthians 2:10, which means "deep, profound and unsearchable wisdom of God, even stress of mind."[5]

Once again, we as Christians especially need to know the truth, the deep and hidden things of God, in order to teach it. Do you agree? If so, let's launch out.

Our studies indicate that Adam was commissioned to work in the Garden of Eden before the fall.[6] His work was to cultivate, which by the Hebrew definition means "to make ready or prepare" the produce of the field.[7] By intuitive reasoning, we can perceive that the produce of the field is simply people of the world, proselytes whom Adam was to care for and to keep safe. The Hebrew definition for the word *keep* means "to preserve, care for, save or protect."[8] Today, we have this same commission, and that is to prepare the way of the Lord, whose kingdom is yet to come as heaven on earth.[9]

The indication here is this: Adam was not the first of the Homo sapiens or such, but rather the first son of God. There is a big difference here because when God breathed into man (Adam), the breath of the Spirit of life, this same man became the first son of God.[10] And who are the sons of God but they who carry the Holy Spirit within them?[11]

From this spiritual realm, God brought Adam down into a deep sleep, even unto the filth of the earth—the dust from which he came.[12] Then God strengthened one of Adam's deficient adversaries (Eve, the rib) who was outside the Garden of Eden and brought her to Adam. Then, rising up together from the dust of the earth according to the will of God, the two became one.[13]

To paraphrase, God took (accepted)[14] a rib(deficient adversary)[15] who existed as a Gentile beside the heavenly realm of Adam and made (raised up, repaired, strengthened, united)[16] the rib, which hesitated (in doubt, limped),[17] into a woman and brought (led)[18] her to Adam. Then God closed up (surrendered, delivered up, secured)[19] the flesh (nakedness, good news, nations)[20] instead (beneath as below the heavens).[21]

The "good news" mentioned here is of the same Hebrew word that is found throughout the New Testament in the word *gospel.*

It's apparent that God so loved the people of the world that the good news of spiritual glory, even for the Gentiles, was sealed up within the marriage of Adam to Eve.

As we launch into the deep with the mind of Christ, common sense, which is united with the Spirit of

God, becomes a reasonable guide that leads us into the righteousness of truth by our faith in the same.[22]

God gave us brains with inherent desire for the knowledge of the truth.[23] And so it is that through ages of incessant study in our universities, we as an intelligent people have learned that mankind was in existence, evolving throughout hundreds and even thousands of years before the coming of Adam, who arrived in approximately 4000 BC. It's also a fact that the ancient Egyptians had a working calendar some three hundred years before the coming of Adam.[24]

Even though the Bible doesn't say it, common sense leads us to believe that Adam and Eve both had to have parents. Jesus did.

Remember what Daniel prophesied: in the end of our current age, knowledge will increase.[25] It is also sensible to understand that we will not achieve unto the knowledge of everything,[26] but we surely don't need to stall out now. Now is the time that God is granting us increased knowledge into the truth for the edification of all mankind, especially for those who are far away. For those who claim to be near, you may not know the truth as you ought to know.[27] We all need to work together in order to establish a peaceful resolution into the kingdom of Jesus that is yet to come.[28] It is written that God has created all peoples, nations, and tongues for His good pleasure, and that all should come and partake of His glory.[29] It's all good.[30]

With the concept in mind that Adam was the first son of God on planet earth, by uniting in marriage with Eve the Gentile, a working biology has produced a certain lineage as a productive vine from the tree of biological life. This lineage, which has increased in the earth, has brought forth the Hebrew people, also known as the Semitic race. The word *Semitic* is derived from the personage of Shem, the son of Noah, a descendant of Adam.[31]

This concept is to be understood upon studying Genesis 10:21. In this passage of scripture we are enlightened to the fact that Shem has become the father or forerunner of all the children of Eber. Now, this word "Eber", according to Hebrew definition, means "Heber" or "Hebrew".[32] This is the foundation name associated with the Jewish nation of Judea because Judea is a name which is founded from the Hebrew tribe of Judah. And the promised Jewish messiah, Jesus, was from the tribe of Judah.[33] And the words Jewish and Judah are synonymous to each other.[34]

As God commissioned Adam to work in the world and to save it (keep it) according to His delight,[35] so also was Noah and his sons commissioned to proselytize (multiply) the world and to draw it back (replenish it) to the righteousness of God's delight that was once established in Eden.[36]

Therefore, in launching out again, it is acceptable to believe that the flood of Noah did not destroy the whole world but rather the whole kingdom of Eden which contained the corrupted descendants of Adam (the first in whom dwelt the breath of the Holy Spirit of life) and those proselytized.

Again, from the beginning, the work of Adam was to proselytize the Gentiles of the world and thereby advance the souls of these people from the likeness or countenance of their primordial roots to the likeness or countenance of the soul of the man Adam and finally into the image of God.

In explanation of this, there is a hierarchy of advancement into the kingdom of God. It works like this.

Unless a person is born from out of the lineage of the Hebrew people, meaning Jewish, the countenance of his or her soul is that of the beasts of the earth known as the Gentile.[37]

There are also lesser life forms upon planet earth that are not associated with the primordial root of the modern Homo sapiens. These are also known as beasts of the earth, or more simply animals.[38]

As for the souls of the Gentiles who have accepted the love of the truth according to the preaching of the sons of God, these have advanced by way of an early spiritual rain from the countenance of the beast of the earth unto likeness of Adam the man. Once God breathes into these the breath of the Holy Spirit of life as a latter spiritual rain, they shall then be advanced into the image of God as adopted sons and daughters of God—and that's after being grafted into the vine of Adam, the first son of God.[39]

This gospel message, which is good news, is given to all races of mankind who are associated with the primordial root of the modern Homo sapiens.[40] This certainly does not apply to lesser life forms, which are truly the beasts of the earth. God is not concerned about oxen, is He?[41]

Therefore it is reasonable to believe that the so-called animals aboard the ark of Noah were selected people of various races who have been proselytized by the sons of Adam in whom dwelt the Holy Spirit of life.[42] These people were selected as male and female who have accepted the good news (gospel message)[43] that was sealed up (secured)[44] in the garden of Eden according the marriage of Adam to Eve the Gentile.[45]

Even so, there were also lesser life forms aboard the ark, and these were for food for the people of God and for a favorable sacrifice at the flood's end.[46]

As the story continues, after the destruction of the flood in which the fountains or pit[47] of the great sea divided,[48] thereby engulfing Eden, the sons of Noah proselytized the surviving nations, which were then called or named after them.[49]

The key word here is *sons*, which by Hebrew definition means "a son or child, offspring, a believer, disciple, follower of, model, likeness, that which is raised up, united, produced, established, bound together, builder of, calf, a lamb, a daughter, etc."[50]

It is therefore apparent that the sons of Noah and the proselytized believers who were aboard the ark after the flood gathered the rest of the known world to which they were sent. Those who were gathered were named after the names of those who called them, being born again according to the work of the sons of Adam, the first son of God.[51]

The first great commission was given to Adam[52] and the second great commission was given to Noah.[53] Even now, the third great commission is given to the modern Church of the true Son of God, Jesus the Savior.[54]

References for Chapter 10

1   Jeremiah 31:31–34. John 1:1–3. Colossians 1:16–17, 3:11.

2   Ecclesiastes 7:1, 8. John 14:6, 18:37.

3   Mark 1:17.

4   Luke 5:4–10 (KJV).

5   Strong's Exhaustive Concordance, Compact Edition, James H. Strong, Baker Book House, Grand Rapids, Michigan, 1984. Pg. 89 of Hebrew dictionary, #5994, 6009. A Complete Hebrew And English Critical And Pronouncing Dictionary, 2nd Edition, William L. Roy, John F. Trow & Co., New York, N.Y. 1846. Pg. 560. Ecclesiastes 1:18.

6   Genesis 2:8, 15.

7   Strong's Exhaustive Concordance, Compact Edition, James H. Strong, Baker Book House, Grand Rapids, Michigan, 1984. Pg. 84 of Hebrew dictionary, #5647–48. A Complete Hebrew And English Critical And Pronouncing Dictionary, 2nd

Edition, William L. Roy, John F. Trow & Co., New York, N.Y. 1846. Pg. 543. Isaiah 60:21, 61:3. Hosea 2:23.

8   Strong's Exhaustive Concordance, Compact Edition. James H. Strong, Baker Book House, Grand Rapids, Michigan, 1984. Pg. 118 of Hebrew dictionary, #8104. A Complete Hebrew And English Critical And Pronouncing Dictionary, 2nd Edition, William L. Roy, John F. Trow & Co., New York, N.Y. 1846. Pg. 678. Matthew 13:23, 38.

9   Isaiah 40:3. Matthew 28:19–20.

10 Genesis 2:7. John 20:21–22.

11 Romans 8:14.

12 A Complete Hebrew And English Critical And Pronouncing Dictionary, 2nd Edition, William L. Roy, John F. Trow & Co., New York, N.Y. 1846. Pg. 563. Genesis 2:7, 21, 18:27. Ezra 6:21, 9:11. Isaiah 26:19. John 6:37–39.

13 Genesis 2:22–25. Isaiah 52:1–2.

14 Strong's Exhaustive Concordance, Compact Edition, James H. Strong, Baker Book House, Grand Rapids, Michigan, 1984. Pg. 60 of Hebrew dictionary, #3947. A Complete Hebrew And English Critical And Pronouncing Dictionary, 2nd Edition, William L. Roy, John F. Trow & Co.,New York, N.Y. 1846. Pg. 416.

15 Strong's Exhaustive Concordance, Compact Edition, James H. Strong, Baker Book House, Grand Rapids, Michigan, 1984. Pg. 100 of Hebrew dictionary, #6761. A Complete Hebrew And English Critical And Pronouncing Dictionary, 2nd Edition, William L. Roy, John F. Trow & Co., New York, N.Y. 1846. Pg. 598.

16 Strong's Exhaustive Concordance, Compact Edition, James H. Strong, Baker Book House, Grand Rapids, Michigan, 1984. Pg. 22 of Hebrew dictionary, #1129. A Complete Hebrew And English Critical And Pronouncing Dictionary, 2nd Edition, William

L. Roy, John F. Trow & Co., New York, N.Y. 1846. Pg. 92, 258.

17 A Complete Hebrew And English Critical And Pronouncing Dictionary, 2nd Edition, William L. Roy, John F. Trow & Co., New York, N.Y. 1846. Pg. 598. Romans 14:23.

18 Strong's Exhaustive Concordance, Compact Edition, James H. Strong, Baker Book House, Grand Rapids, Michigan, 1984. Pg. 19 of Hebrew dictionary, #935. A Complete Hebrew And English Critical And Pronouncing Dictionary, 2nd Edition, William L. Roy, John F. Trow & Co., New York, N.Y. 1846. Pg. 59.

19 Strong's Exhaustive Concordance, Compact Edition, James H. Strong, Baker Book House, Grand Rapids, Michigan, 1984. Pg. 82 of Hebrew dictionary, #5462. A Complete Hebrew And English Critical And Pronouncing Dictionary, 2nd Edition, William L. Roy, John F. Trow & Co., New York, N.Y. 1846. Pg. 533.

20 Strong's Exhaustive Concordance, Compact Edition, James H. Strong, Baker Book House, Grand Rapids, Michigan, 1984. Pg. 24 of Hebrew dictionary, #1319–20. A Complete Hebrew And English Critical And Pronouncing Dictionary, 2nd Edition, William L. Roy, John F. Trow & Co., New York, N.Y. 1846. Pg. 116.

21 Strong's Exhaustive Concordance, Compact Edition, James H. Strong, Baker Book House, Grand Rapids, Michigan, 1984. Pg. 124 of Hebrew dictionary, #8478–79. A Complete Hebrew And English Critical And Pronouncing Dictionary, 2nd Edition, William L. Roy, John F. Trow & Co., New York, N.Y. 1846. Pg. 705. Genesis 2:21-22 (KJV).

22 Psalm 85:11–13. Proverbs 8:6–9. John 16:13. 1 Corinthians 2:7, 16. 2 Thessalonians 2:13.

23 Job 36:22, 38:36. Psalm 51:6. Proverbs 2:6. Daniel 2:20–22.

24 The American Peoples Encyclopedia, A Modern Reference Work, Grolier Incorporated, New York, N.Y. 1965. Vol. 4, Pg. 118.

25 Daniel 12:4.

26 Ecclesiastes 8:17.

27 1 Corinthians 8:1–2.

28 Ephesians 2:13–18.

29 Strong's Exhaustive Concordance, Compact Edition, James H. Strong, Baker Book House, Grand Rapids, Michigan, 1984. Pg. 110 of Hebrew dictionary, #7522. Numbers 14:21. Psalms 86:9–10. Revelation 4:11 (KJV), 5:9–10, 15:4.

30 Genesis 1:31.

31 American Peoples Encyclopedia, A Modern Reference Work, Grolier Incorporated, New York, N.Y. 1965. Vol.10, Pg. 521. Genesis 10:21.

32 Strong's Exhaustive Concordance, Compact Edition, James H. Strong, Baker Book House, Grand Rapids, Michigan, 1984. Pg. 85 of Hebrew dictionary, #5677, 5680. A Complete Hebrew And

English Critical And Pronouncing Dictionary, 2nd Edition, William L. Roy, John F. trow & Co., New York, N.Y. 1846. Pg. 544.

33 Isaiah 9:6-7. Micah 5:2.

34 Strong's Exhaustive Concordance, Compact Edition, James H. Strong, Baker Book House, Grand Rapids, Michigan, 1984. Pg. 47 of Hebrew dictionary, #3063–64. A Complete Hebrew And English Critical And Pronouncing Dictionary, 2nd Edition, William L. Roy, John F. Trow & Co., New York, N.Y. 1846. Pg. 266.

35 Strong's Exhaustive Concordance, Compact Edition, James H. Strong, Baker book House, Grand Rapids, Michigan, 1984. Pg. 84 of Hebrew dictionary, #5647, Pg. 118 of Hebrew dictionary, #8104. Genesis 2:15 (KJV).

36 Strong's Exhaustive Concordance, Compact Edition, James H. Strong, baker Book House, Grand Rapids, Michigan, 1984. Pg. 106 of Hebrew

dictionary, #7235, Pg. 66 of Hebrew dictionary, #4390. Genesis 9:1.

37 Strong's Exhaustive Concordance, Compact Edition, James H. Strong, Baker Book House, Grand Rapids, Michigan, 1984. Pg. 26 of Hebrew dictionary, #1471.

38 Strong's Exhaustive Concordance, Compact Edition, James H. Strong, Baker Book House, Grand Rapids, Michigan, 1984. Pg. 19 of Hebrew dictionary, #929–30. A Complete Hebrew And English Critical And Pronouncing Dictionary, 2nd Edition, William L. Roy, John F. Trow & Co., New York, N.Y. 1846. Pg. 68–69.

39 Genesis 1:26. Joel 2:22–23. John 1:12, 20:21–22. Romans 11:17–24.

40 Joel 2:28.

41 1 Corinthians 9:9.

42 Genesis 6:7, 17–20.

43 See Reference 20.

44 See Reference 20.

45 Genesis 2:21–22.

46 Genesis 6:21, 8:20.

47 A Complete Hebrew And English Critical And Pronouncing Dictionary, 2nd Edition, William L. Roy, John F. Trow & Co., New York, N.Y. 1846. Pg. 553.

48 Strong's Exhaustive Concordance, Compact Edition, James H. Strong, Baker Book House, Grand Rapids, Michigan, 1984. Pg. 23 of Hebrew dictionary, #1234. A Complete Hebrew And English Critical And Pronouncing Dictionary, 2nd Edition, William L. Roy, John F. Trow & Co., New York, N.Y. 1846. Pg. 105. Genesis 7:11.

49 Genesis 9:1–2, 7.

50 Strong's Exhaustive Concordance, Compact Edition, James H. Strong, Baker Book House, Grand Rapids, Michigan, 1984. Pg. 21–22 of Hebrew dictionary, #1121. A complete Hebrew And English Critical Pronouncing Dictionary, 2nd Edition, William L.

Roy, John F. Trow & Co., New York, N.Y. 1846. Pg. 92–93.

51 Genesis 2:19–20, 10:1.

52 Genesis 2:15, 3:23.

53 Genesis 9:1

54 Matthew 28:18–20. Mark 16:15–16. John 1:34, 3:16–18. 1 John 4:14–15.

In Summary

As discussed earlier, all of mankind must be born again—not should be, but *must* be born again. Jesus broke this rebirth concept down into two spiritual steps. One is to be born of the water of life, and the other is to be born of the Spirit of God.[1]

First and foremost, all of mankind must be born of or transformed into the water of life. By the Hebrew definition, the word *water* indicates the semen of a living seed that flows through the lineage of Abraham, Isaac, and Jacob.[2]

As Jesus instructed the woman at the well, saying, "Salvation is of the Jews," it becomes evident that one who is not a Jew must be transformed into or reborn spiritually as a Jew. God swore unto Abraham, saying, "In Isaac, thy seed, shall all the nations of the world shall be blessed."[3]

Isaac, who is the seed of Abraham, brought forth Jacob, whose descendants have become the Jewish nation of Israel. From out of the Jewish nation of Israel has come forth the promise of abundant prosperity and happiness in the personage of Jesus the Jew. This same Jesus has become the God-sent Messiah or Savior of all mankind which exists within the sorrows of darkness and alienation from the light and goodness of God. This applies to both Jew and Gentile alike, for it is written, "Yet, the number of the children of Israel shall be as the sand of the sea, which cannot be measured or numbered, and it shall come to pass, that in the place where it is said unto them, you are not my people, there it will be said unto them, you are the sons of the living God."[4]

As Brother Paul put it, the Gentiles have become adopted sons and daughters of God as joint heirs with the Jews, being grafted into the vine of Adam through the seed of Abraham by faith in Jesus.[5] Therefore the Gentiles have become spiritual Jews.

As it is, Abraham himself was a descendant (offspring) of the seed of Adam. According to Hebrew semantics, the term "offspring or seed of Adam" simply means "son of man."[6] Therefore when a Gentile becomes born of the water by receiving this seed as an early rain of the spirit of Jesus, he or she becomes known as a "son of man" or Jewish person.

Remember that Jesus, who is the true Son of God, also referred to Himself as the Son of man, for He was of Jewish lineage from the tribe of Judah, a descendant of Adam, the man.[7]

According to biblical teachings, all of mankind, whether Jew or Gentile, who have received of the early rain of the spirit of the Son of man shall then receive of the latter rain of the spirit of the Son of God, and they'll advance into a kingdom of priests upon the earth.[8] This advancement is predicated after the order of Melchizedek.[9]

Now, what does this mean, and who is Melchizedek?

According to the Book of Genesis, Melchizedek was a minister of the oracles of the Most-High God, but where did he come from?[10] An acceptable answer to this question is documented in the Book of Jasher.

According to our modern canon of the Bible, this book is considered non-canonical, but it was included in the work of Esdras, a priest of Babylonian captivity (560–491 BC) who put in order the foundation books of our now accepted Old Testament. His work included the Pentateuch and also the Book of Jasher in a non-corrupted form.[11] Even though it is now considered non-canonical, and probably because it surfaced so late in literary history, its existence is recognized twice in our modern Bible.[12]

It is in this book that Melchizedek who is called (king of righteousness), is called Adonizedek (lord of righteousness). This same person is indeed Shem, the son of Noah.[13]

This passage gives credence to what we have discussed in the last chapter and is associated with Genesis 10:21. Out of Shem comes the lineage of the Hebrew people.

There is a mystery here. When Gentiles accept the love of the truth that is in Jesus, they become spiritual Jews and are advanced into a kingdom of priests and adopted sons and daughters of God after the order of Melchizedek, the priest of the Most-High God and the forerunner of the Hebrew Jewish nation.[14]

In continuing onward, the first step toward the light of salvation, whether Jew or Gentile, is to accept God's provision for salvation, which exists only in His Son Jesus. After this, there is a certain period of growth that occurs as discussed in the parable of the sower and the seed.[15]

If a person's heart is good, after the promised seed

is sown, it shall produce fruit. This fruit is in truth the Holy Spirit, which gives life unto all who believe.[16]

This takes us to the second and final step to being born again, and that is being born of the spirit.

As discussed earlier, the mystery of our church age was established in the Garden of Eden, when the good news (gospel) of Gentile acceptance occurred at the marriage of Adam to Eve.[17] As the story goes, Adam, who was the first son of God, became one with Eve according to acceptance. And so it is now that Jesus, the true Son of God, becomes one with the Gentile— again, only according to acceptance.[18]

This concept of Jesus being one with all of mankind, according to acceptance, is for both Jew and Gentile alike. Jesus came unto His own (Jewish lineage), but His own did not accept Him. Any person, whether Jew or Gentile, who accepts Him is given the right to become the sons and daughters of God who first and foremost accept the living water of Jesus, the true Son of God.[19]

The analogy here is this: when the seed of Adam, which was with Eve, entered into her, Eve became the mother of all the living.[20] And so it is now that the Spirit of Jesus, who is with us, shall enter into us.[21] Thus, we shall become the sons and daughters of God among the living because it is the Spirit of God in unity with Jesus that gives life.[22]

Remember that when God breathed the breath of life into Adam (the man), he became a living soul that we understand to be the first son of God.[23] This same event has occurred in the early New Testament Church, when Jesus breathed the breath of life into His disciples, saying, "Receive the Holy Spirit."[24] Those who patiently wait and therefore receive the power of the Holy Spirit shall be called the sons of the living God.[25]

To believe in Jesus is to be "born of the water" (the early rain). To receive the Holy Spirit is to be "born of the spirit" (the latter rain). This fulfills the requirement of "You must be born again."[26]

Therefore whether you are a Jew or Gentile, come to

the waters and receive the showers of the blessings of eternal life that are without money and without cost.[27]

Sincerely to all,

Frank Ovec

References for Summary

1 John 3:3–8.

2 Strong's Exhaustive Concordance, Compact Edition, James H. Strong, Baker Book House, Grand Rapids, Michigan, 1984. Pg. 65 of Hebrew dictionary, #4325. Exodus 3:6. Luke 20:37–38.

3 Genesis 17:19, 21:12, 22:17–18. John 4:22.

4 Hosea 1:10.

5 Romans 8:15–23, 11:13–20. Galatians 3:26–29. Ephesians 1:5. 2 Timothy 3:14–15.

6 Strong's Exhaustive Concordance, Compact Edition, James H. Strong, Baker Book House, Grand Rapids, Michigan, 1984. Pg. 21 of Hebrew dictionary, #1121. Pg. 36 of Hebrew dictionary, #2232–34. A Complete Hebrew And English Critical And Pronouncing Dictionary, 2nd Edition, William L. Roy, John F. Trow & Co., New York, N.Y. 1846. Pg. 14 and 223.

7 Matthew 12:40, 16:13–16, 17:9–12. Luke 1:35, 9:22.

8 Hosea 6:3. Joel 2:23. Zechariah 10:1. John 1:11–13, 14:17. Revelation 5:9–10.

9 Psalm 110:4

10 Genesis 14:18.

11 Introduction and Preface of "The Book Of Jasher", Noah And Gould Publishing Co., New York, N.Y. 1840. From the translation of Albinus Alcuin. 800 AD.

12 Josuha 10:13. 2 Samuel 1:18.

13 The Book Of Jasher, Noah And Gould Publishing Co.,New York, N.Y. 1840. From the translation of Albinus Alcuin. 800 AD. Pg. 45. Genesis 14:18. Hebrews 7:1–2.

14 Psalm 110:4.

15 Matthew 13:1–23. Luke 8:4–15.

16 John 6:63. Galatians 3:6–9, 14–18, 26–29.

17 See Chapter 10 of this book. Genesis 2:23–24. Ephesians 5:30–32.

18 Genesis 2:7, 2:21–24. Galatians 3:28.

19 John 1:11–13, 4:10,14.

20 Genesis 3:20.

21 John 14:17.

22 John 6:63, 10:30.

23 Genesis 2:7. John 1:12. Romans 8:11–14.

24 Luke 3:16. John 20:21–22.

25 Hosea 1:10. John 1:12, 32–34. Acts 1:8, 2:38–39.
Romans 8:14.

26 John 3:5–7.

27 Isaiah 55:1–3. Ezekial 34:25–31.

Printed in the United States
by Baker & Taylor Publisher Services